INTEGRITY & HONOR...

A Faith-Based Coloring Book for Those Who Love a First Responder

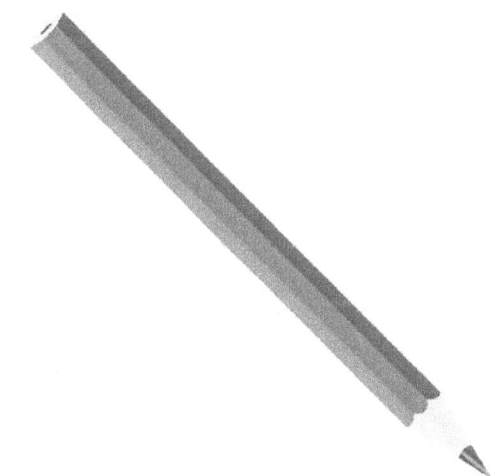

By: Kristi Neace

(Insert Your Own Doodle Here)

Copyright Kristi Neace, 2017
All Rights Reserved
Printed in the United States of America
By: CreateSpace.com
ISBN-13: 978-1979305983

Under International Copyright Law, no part of this publication may be reproduced, stored, or transmitted by any means – electronic, mechanical, photographic (photocopy), recording, or otherwise – without written permission from the author.

Illustrations may not be reproduced without prior consent.

Welcome to my new adventure, a coloring book for those who love a first responder or *are* the responder sent out to serve. I have designed these color pages from my own experiences of living this life for over 30 years.

With each picture, there is a thought provoking passage aimed at encouraging *you* the color artist.

Though the pictures are not perfect, nor the words as poetic as I would love them to be, I pray that somehow they will touch your heart and leave you to realize that you are loved…you are appreciated…and you have purpose!

Many blessings, friend. I hope you enjoy!

Kristi

To God…Thank You for letting me use the gifts You have given me. This one has been so fun!

Trust in the LORD with all your heart and lean not on your own understanding; in all your ways submit to him, and he will make your paths straight. – Proverbs 3:5-6

Trust in the Lord...a simple phrase we sometimes hear, but fail to put into practice. Is God really trustworthy? Does He care about me and my family? Why does it seem as if bad things still happen to good people?

First of all, the Bible tells us that God is "good". This means that He is the exact opposite of "bad". He is a *good* Father – gentle and loving towards His children, but also a fair disciplinarian to those who are not walking according to His will.

A *good* father is trustworthy, and our Heavenly Father is exactly that – trust...worthy. He cares deeply for you and me, yet we live in a world marred by the ugliness of sinful choices and behaviors. Because of this, "good" people often find themselves caught up in the ripple effects of the poor choices of others, and even those of their own.

As the wife and the mom of a police officer, I have to give my men over to the Lord every day. There is nothing in *my* power that can keep them safe or protect their steps in the midst of all the bad, therefore, my heart says something like this each day in my prayers to God...

Lord, I trust You and ask You to protect my husband/my son/my son-in-law from harm today on their shift. Use them to do good and to help those who are at their weakest moments. Give them courage to answer the difficult calls. Protect their mind from any hint of darkness the enemy may try and sow there. Help them to always remember who they are in You and draw them close. Finally, Lord, keep <u>my</u> mind steadfast, <u>my</u> eyes affixed and <u>my</u> heart immovable. May I have the courage to fight the battles on the home front as my warriors fight abroad. Amen.

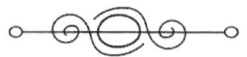

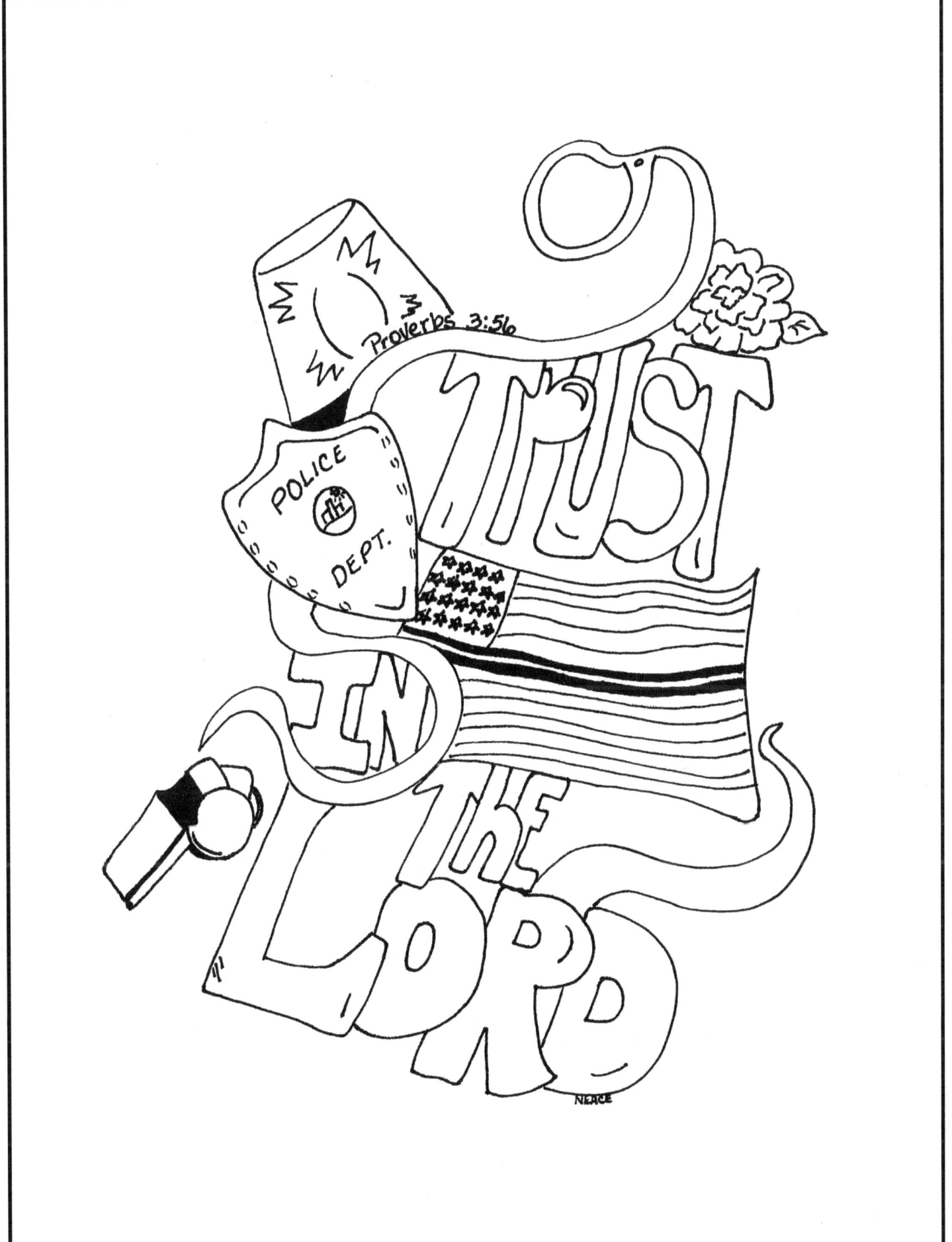

Always Kiss Your Cop Goodnight...what a great reminder! With all the busyness of being a wife, a mom, a homemaker, a business woman, a chauffeur, coach, referee, Mimi, etc., sometimes our "other half" gets pushed to the bottom of our to-do list. Yet, it is *vital* that we keep the flame stoked within our marital relationship.

Have you ever sat by a crackling fire? It doesn't take long for the flames to lap their way right through a piece of wood until a chunk breaks off and rolls a slight distance away. As you watch, the embers on that broken piece stay lit for just a small window of time, and it is inevitable that if the log is not returned to the flame, the fire will die out and leave a blackened remnant of what once was.

Today, guard your marriage and keep the embers lit. Our marriage is a gift from God and we must do whatever we can to help guard it from becoming another burnt out statistic. So, love with all your might. Be cognizant of your time making sure your spouse or significant other feels important. Be your officer's biggest cheerleader. In the end, the love you have for one another will only grow stronger.

So what are you waiting for? Go kiss that cop of yours goodnight!

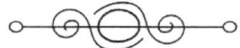

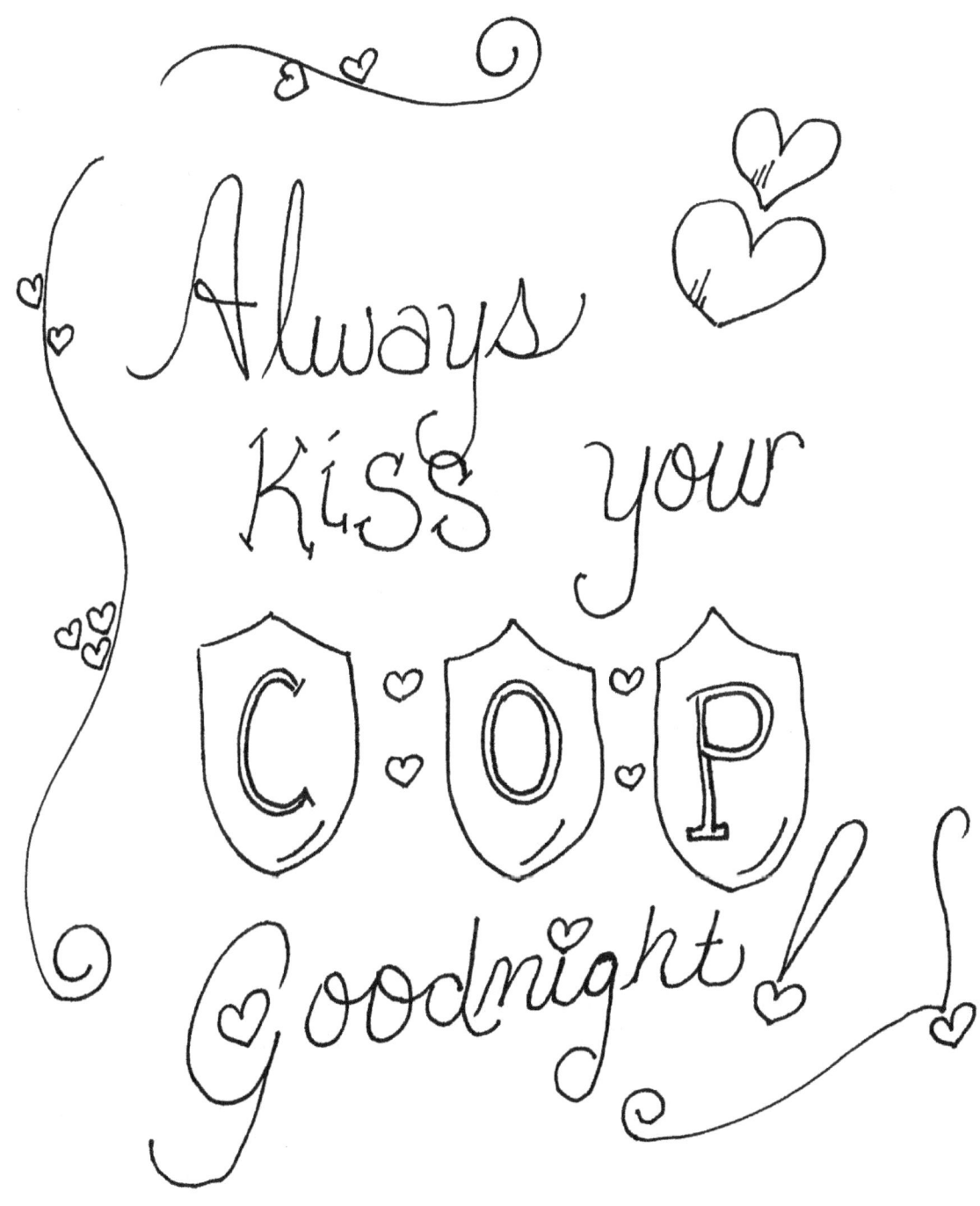

I keep my eyes always on the LORD. With him at my right hand, I will not be shaken. – Psalm 16:8

I Will Not Be Shaken... law enforcement life is not for the faint of heart. It takes patience, understanding, a generous amount of love, and a large portion of grace, but this I know, no matter what life throws at me, I will not be shaken by it.

There's a story in the Bible about a man who built his home upon a rock. When the winds blew and the rains came down, the home stood strong. Another man, however, built his home upon the sand. When the winds blew and the rains came down, his house crumbled.

Today, I don't know what you have built your "house" on, but as for me and my household, we will serve the Lord, and because of His great grace towards us, our home will stand!

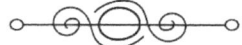

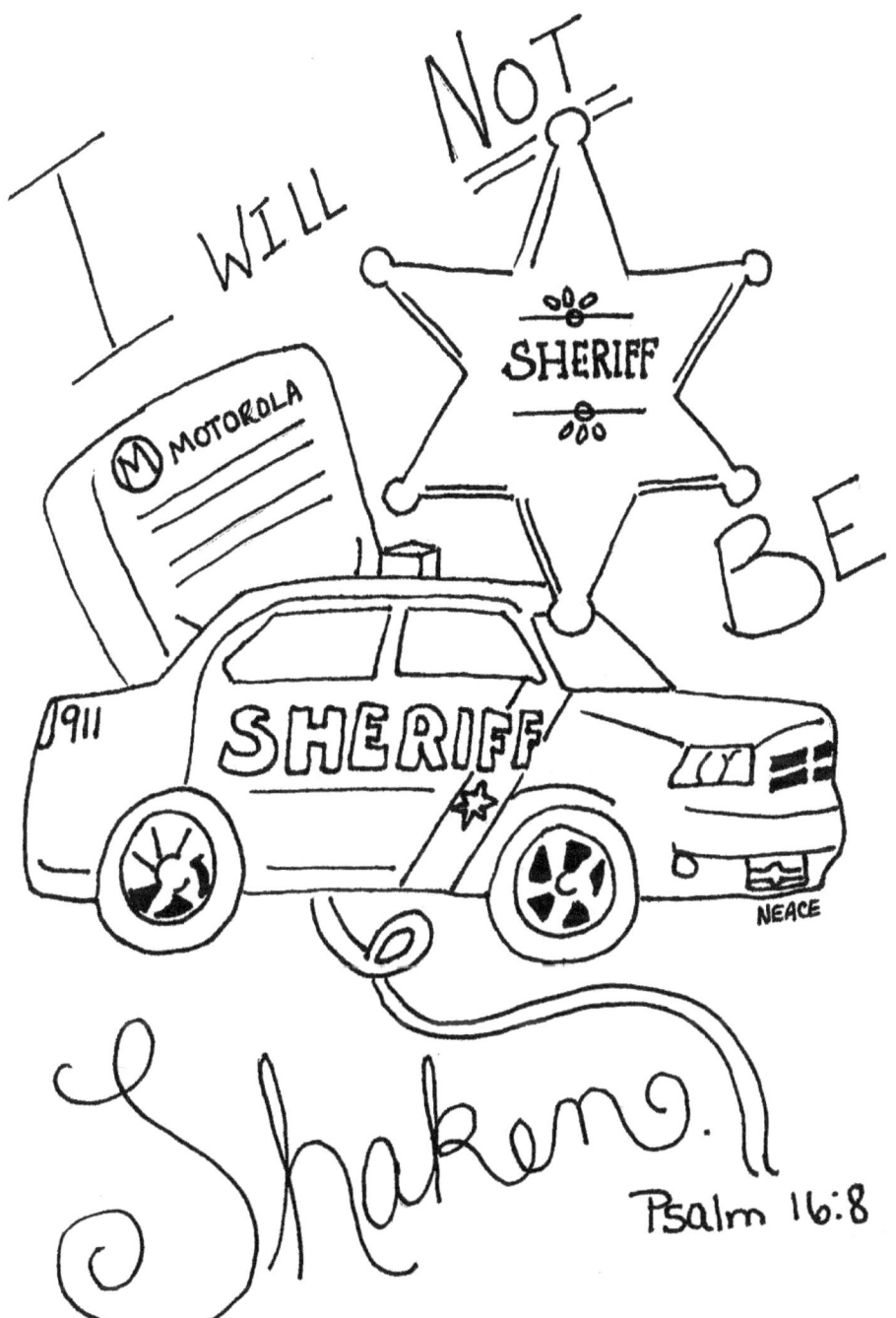

Come Home Safe!!... How many times have I strained to hear the car door slam in front of the house, then a turn of the knob? Too many to count, I assure you. Being married to the badge, there is always that thought in the back of your mind…"Will he come home?" To me, however, I choose not to focus on the "what ifs," but rather the "What I knows".

I know I love him and have made every effort to display that love when we are together.

I know he is doing what he is called to do and does it well.

I know his training has been extensive, and he is mindful of his surroundings at all times.

I know that he would rather be home than pulling that extra shift, but because he is a good provider, he is going the extra mile.

I know that if anything were to happen, God would supply my need as I maneuvered that journey forward.

And finally, I know that when he walks through the door, I can breathe a little easier, for he's safe.

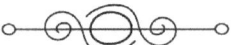

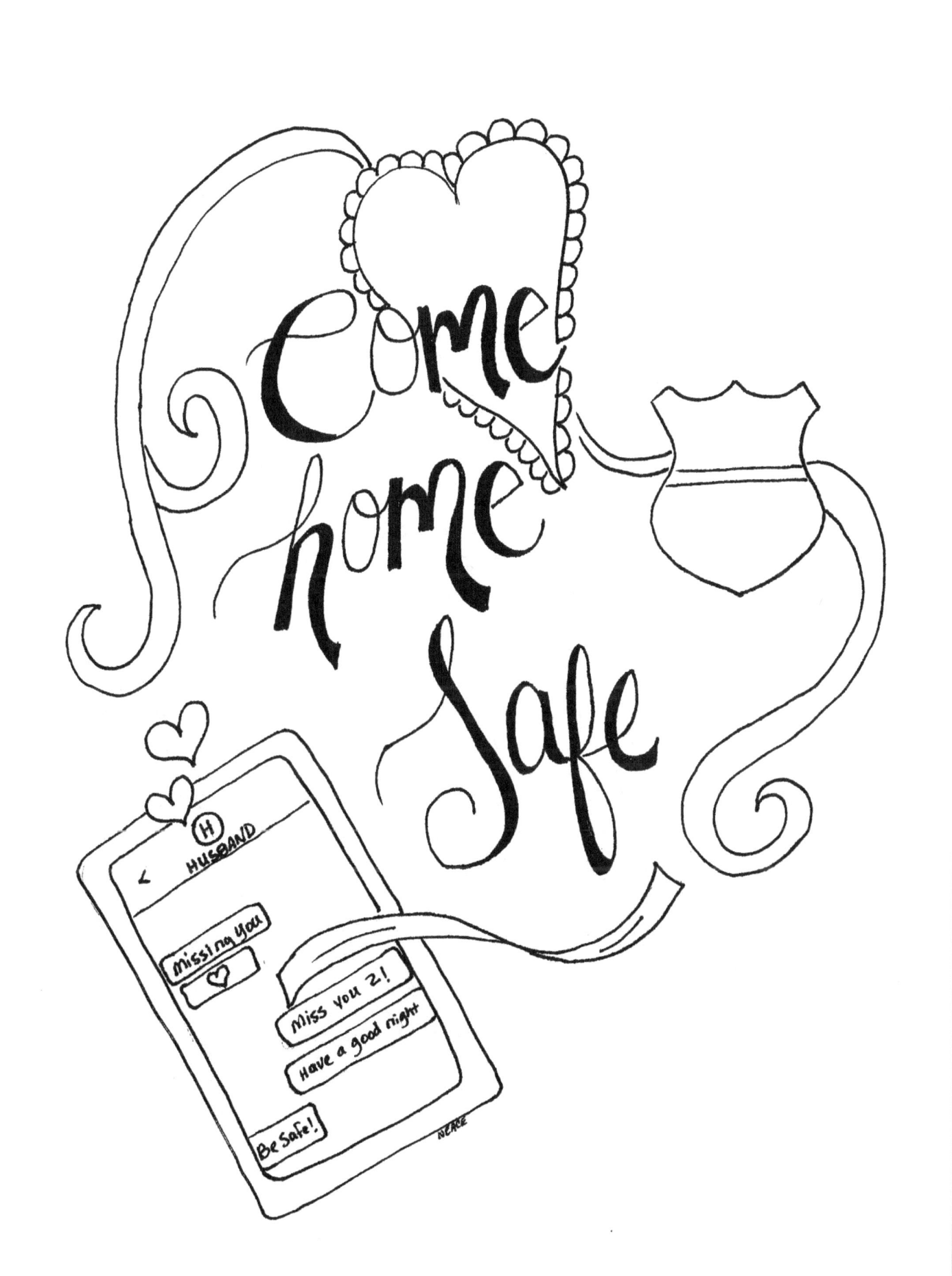

Praise be to the LORD my Rock, who trains my hands for war, my fingers for battle. Psalm 144:1

Hands for War, Fingers for Battle…

We don't like to think that our officers are going off to war each day, but that is exactly what is happening. Whether or not they ever face a gun fight, they are continuously bombarded by ammunition of the enemy through assaults of the mind, the psyche, physically, and most detrimental - spiritually. They are at war, yet we take great peace in knowing they have been called and trained up by the Lord, Himself, to handle each battle that heads their direction.

Today, let us see the fervency in active battle on behalf of these warriors through daily prayers. Join me in praying…

Dear Gracious Heavenly Father,
We come to You and ask that You place your garment of protection over each of our officers. That You give them a belt of truth to hold them together when things seem to unravel. Give them a vest of righteousness, so they will cling to what is good and reject that which is not of You. Please bless them with shoes of peace that bring comfort in any situation. May they have a shield, or badge of faith that continuously reminds them Who they are actually serving, and finally, give them a helmet of salvation that they may fight with confidence knowing they belong to You!
Thank you, Lord. Amen.

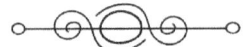

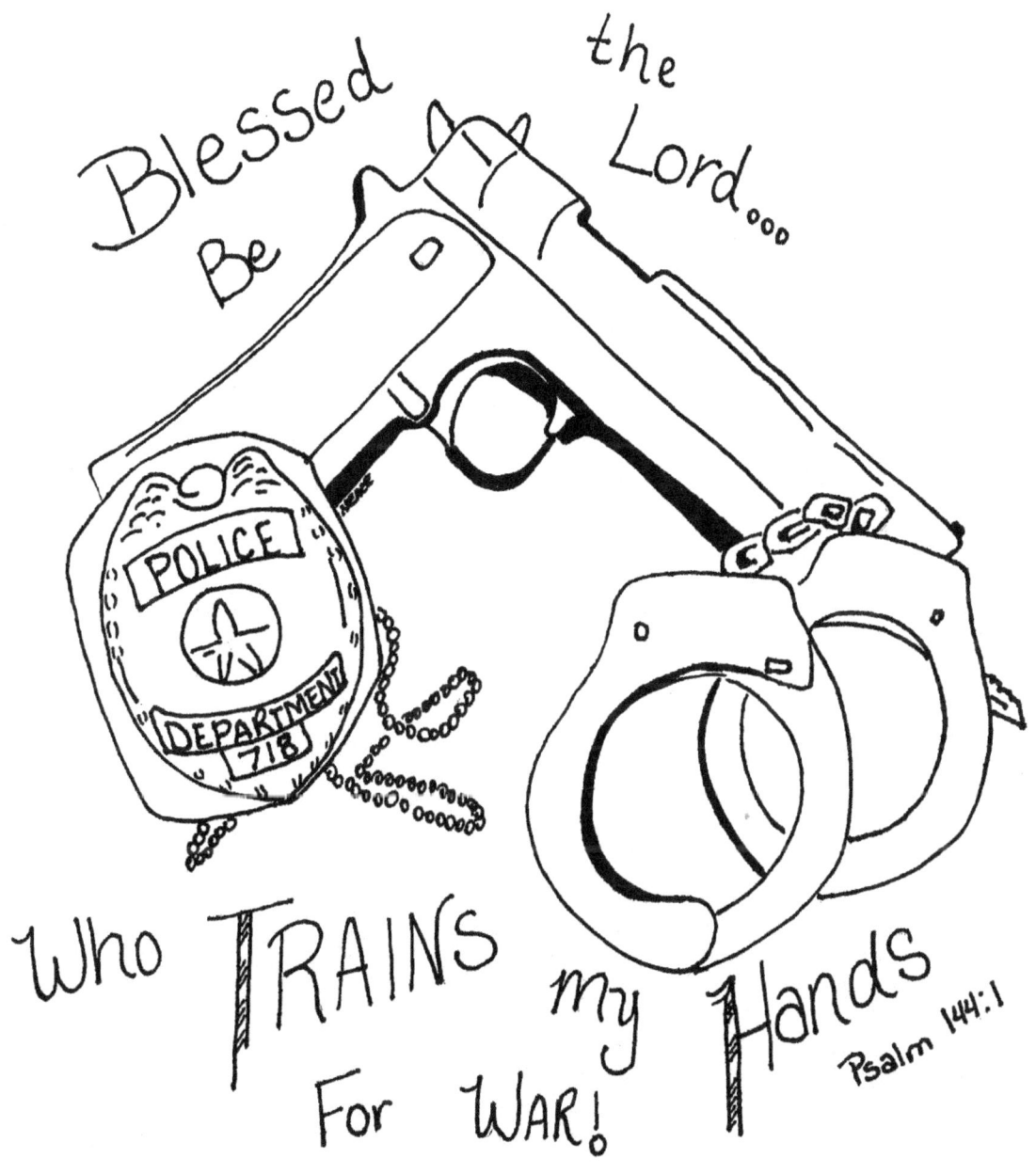

Integrity & Honor...

These are two words which seem to be harder to find these days. Yet, I am thankful we still have men and women who serve with these on the forefront of their minds; those homeland warriors who set aside their own safety for the safety of others. They leave all that is sacred and comfortable in order to stare down the ugliness of this world, and they do it with quality that sets an example for us all.

Integrity – doing the right thing even when no-one notices or recognizes the contribution; being honest and having strong moral principles.

Honor – being highly respected because of his or her respectable character; having a distinction above the rest.

What a privilege it is to share life with an officer. They are head and shoulders above the rest!

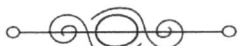

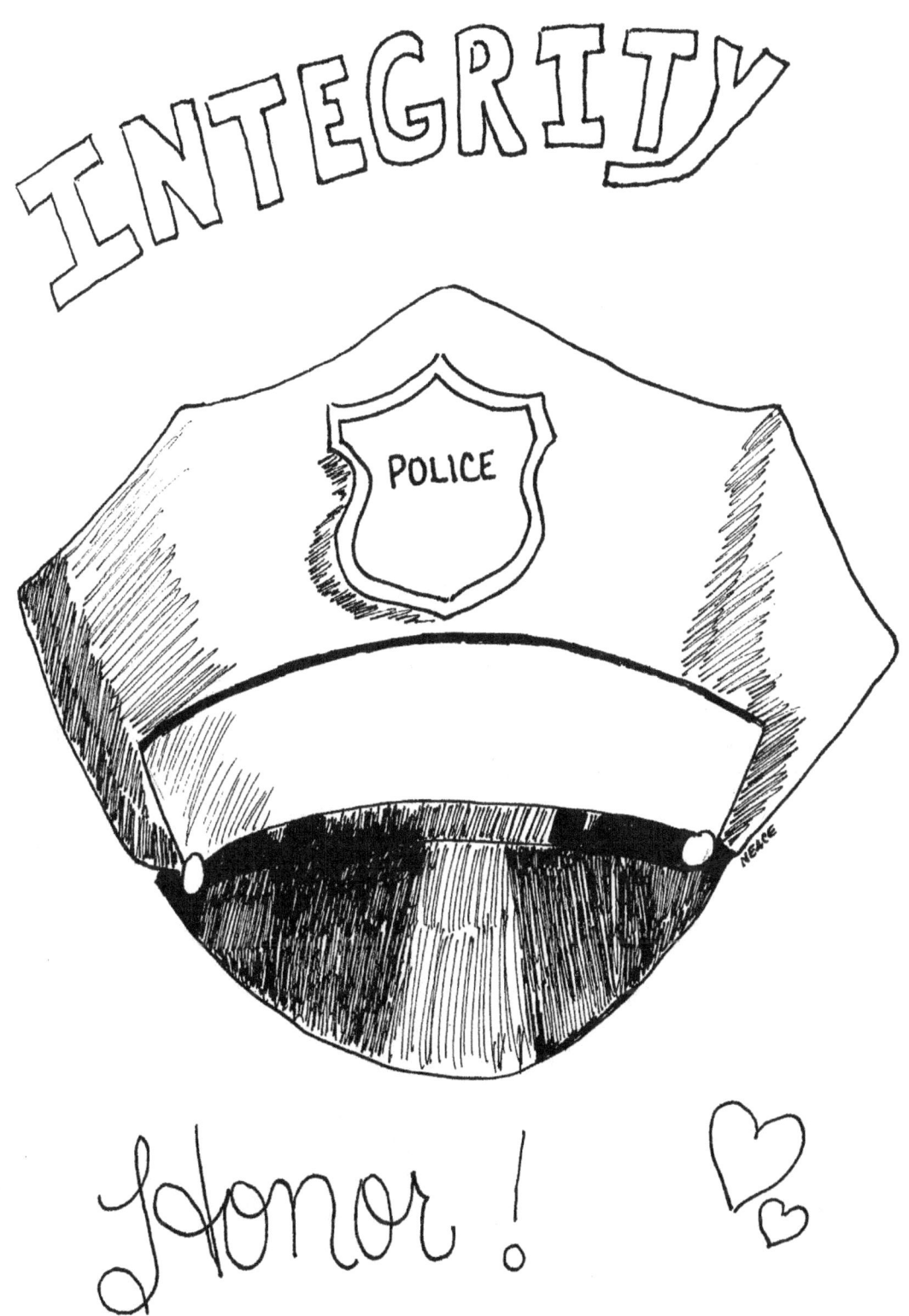

Therefore what God has joined together, let no one separate. – Mark 10:9

What God has joined...

Did you realize that your marriage is God ordained? Yes! The Lord is the Author and Perfector of the marital institution. Therefore, we must make every effort to keep it vibrant and wholesome in the sight of the Lord.

There will be times when life gets in the way, when we are busy working, being mom and dad, balancing the pressures of life. Those are the times, however, we need to make every effort to reconnect as a couple and seek God's will for our relationship. Why do we see so many divorces in this profession? Because we allow the stresses to take a front seat in our marriage; we put "self" in the driver's seat, and place unhealthy expectations on our spouse. Because they are human, they fail us and we become disillusioned. Yet, God will never fail us, for *He* alone is perfect.

Today, let's pray that God will help refocus our attention onto Him, and seek to love our mate the way He intended.

Dear Heavenly Father,
Thank you for my marriage. Help me to cherish it and groom it to be all that You want it to be. Help me to not place unfair expectations on my spouse, but find my worth and my purpose in You alone. I love You, Lord. Amen.

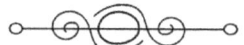

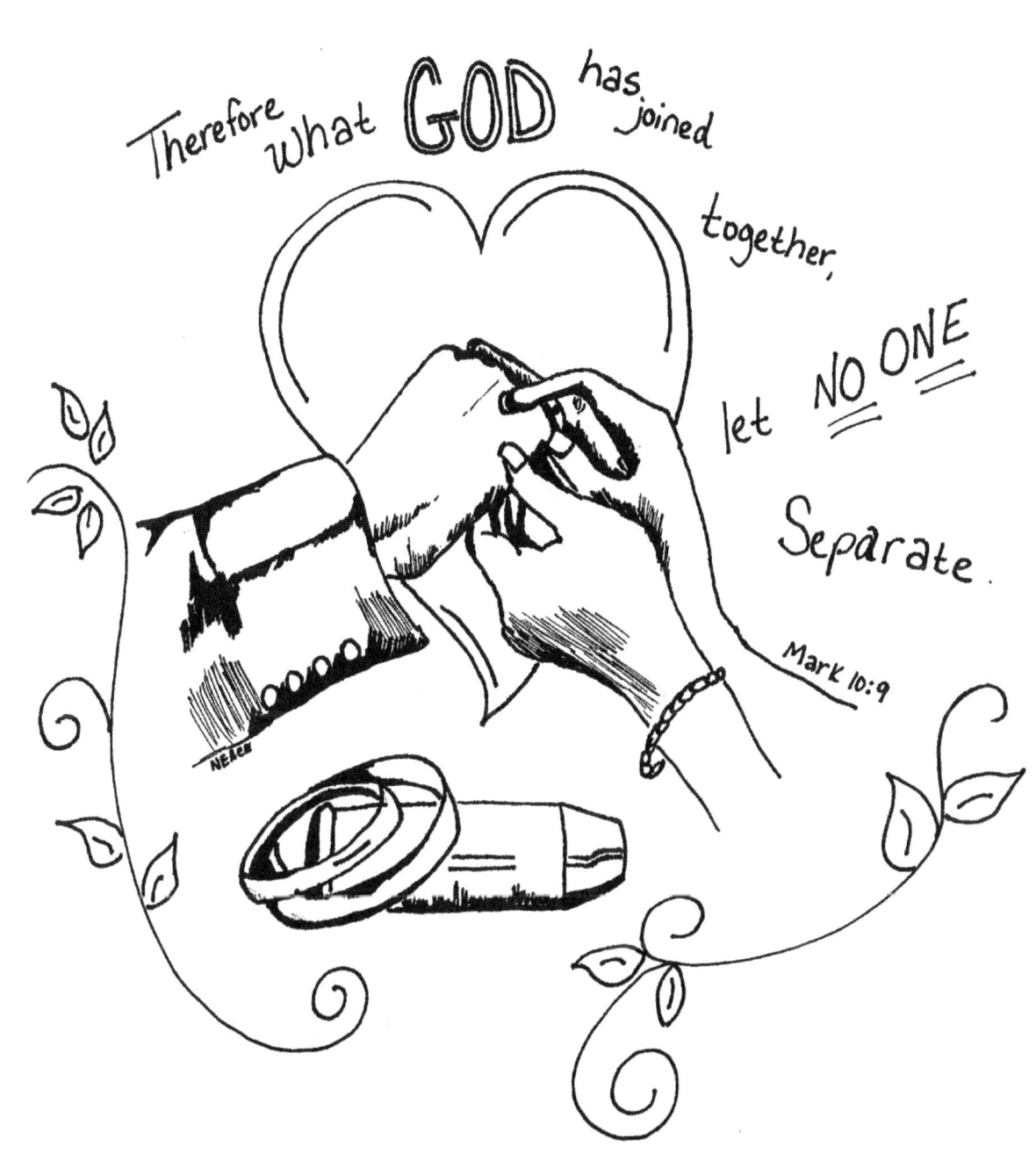

Family. Do Not Cross!...

I remember when I was growing up, there was a ceramic napkin holder which sat on our dining room table. It had a pair of praying hands on the front along with these words: *The Family that Prays Together, Stays Together.*

This blue family is a tight community of folks and we, for the most part, believe in the strength of family. It is one of those sacred things, and anyone who tries to come against it is not looked upon favorably.

Yet…sometimes we allow the job, our own selfish desires, hobbies, or other things somehow slip in and begin damaging and diminishing the family unit.

Today, make sure you do your part to protect what God has given, and may we all stand firm as defenders through prayer and togetherness.

This family…may nothing cross it that is unwanted, ungodly, or unhealthy.

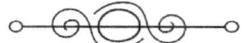

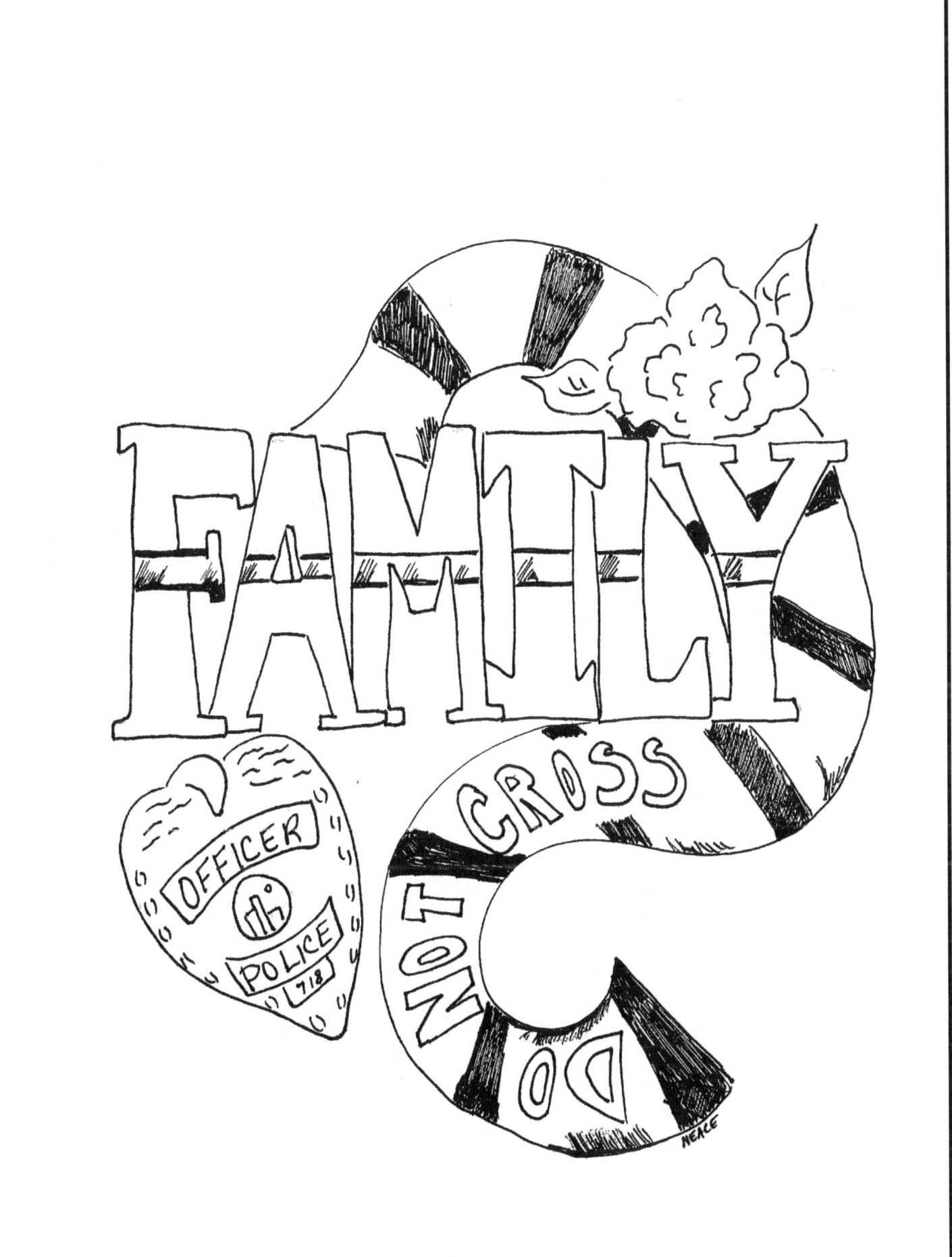

For the one in authority is God's servant for your good. But if you do wrong, be afraid, for rulers do not bear the sword for no reason. They are God's servants, agents of wrath to bring punishment on the wrongdoer. – Romans 13:4

God's Servant...

What a novel idea! We don't usually think of a law enforcement officer as a servant of God, but that is what he or she truly is!

I once read something that said if cops were not cops, they would be ministers. Why is that? Because they have a servant's heart. It is in their DNA to serve and sacrifice, to help and protect others. These qualities are the same qualities God develops within ministers.

According to Romans 13, our officers are raised up and put into place by God in order to promote peace and keep boundaries in check.

Yet, those who choose to ignore or otherwise cross those boundaries, often find themselves in a place of judgment by the very ones who are there for their good. May we always uphold the laws God has established, and especially hold in high esteem those who are placed there to protect them.

Dear Gracious Heavenly Father,
Thank You for our law enforcement. Thank You for raising up these brave men and women to serve as defenders and protectors of our land and law. May they be strengthened and encouraged today as they serve. Amen.

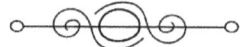

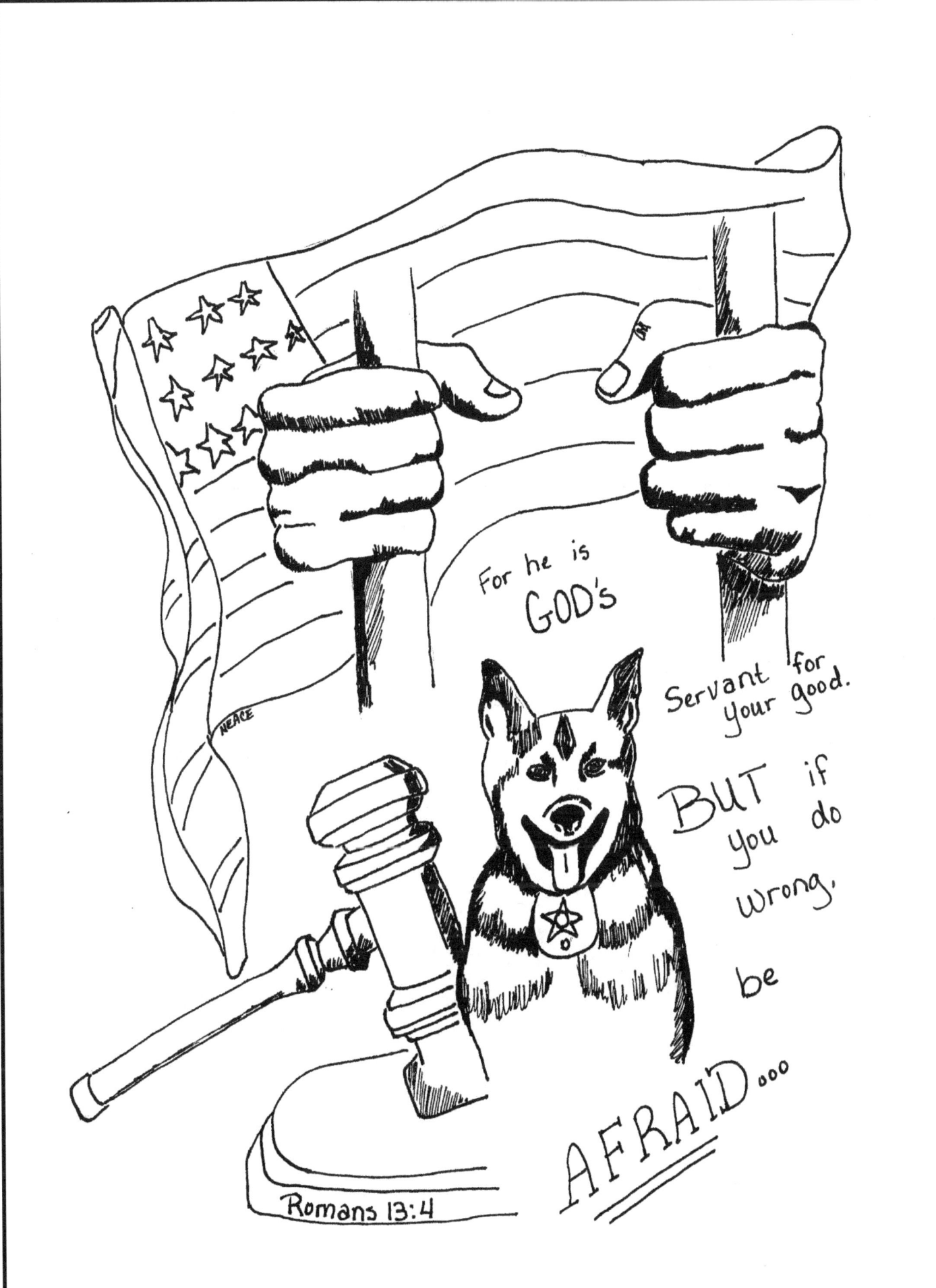

A Firefighter's Flame...

Ever before my husband was a cop, he was a volunteer fireman. I remember many date nights we ran code to brush fires, car fires, or whatever else he may be needed at, and especially memorable, was the time I was left directing traffic while my man suited up and headed in. Nothing says romance like a good whiff of smoke from a blazing, out-of-control fire. ☺

Of course, as with law enforcement or any other type of emergency service, the spouse plays a vital role in the well-being of the responder. It is no secret that these types of positions can suck the life out of the ones fighting the battles, and devastating situations they find themselves in can leave a lasting mark on their well being. Yet, a wonderfully in-tune spouse can help to alleviate stresses and bring some semblance of normalcy in these active households.

Stay the course, my friend. You are a vital part of a successful responder!

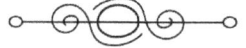

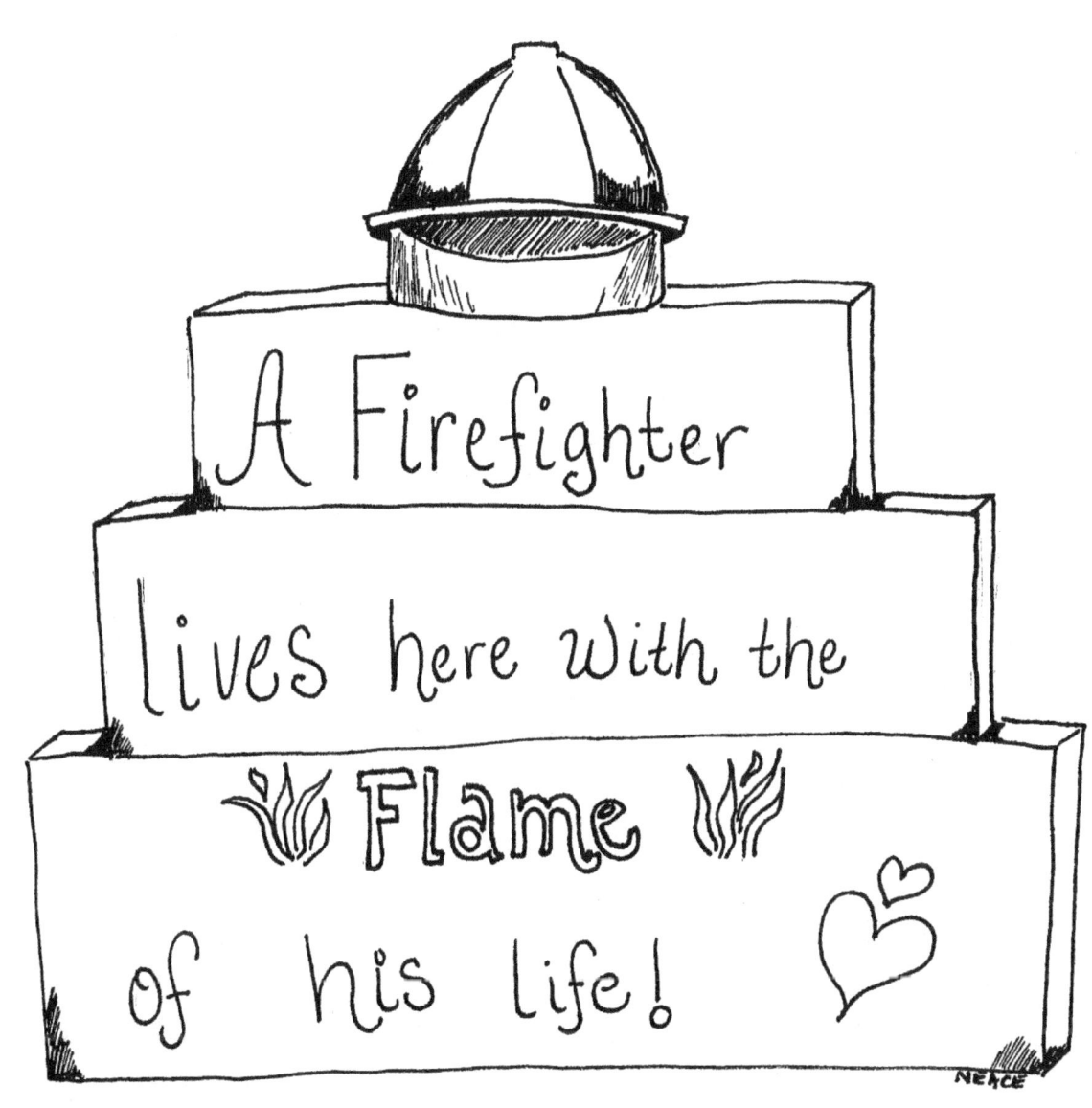

...we went through fire and water, but you brought us to a place of abundance. – Psalm 66:12b

Through the Fire...

There are times in each of our lives that we walk through difficult situations. The way will often seem dark and perilous. Perhaps we are facing a disease, a financial crisis, a divorce, the death of a loved one, or whatever it might be, and we have no idea how we are going to make it through.

Just as a firefighter suits up and meets the flames head on confident that his or her equipment and training will help them get the job done, we, too, can suit up by putting on God's spiritual armor, seek His will and strength through training of His Word, and rest in the fact that God will be with us through the fire. There will come a point in time when we can sit around and tell stories of God's goodness through the harrowing experience of the trial. So, be encouraged! Your God will walk you through even the hottest blaze.

Dear Gracious Heavenly Father,
Thank You for being with me through the trials of life. Help me to continuously prepare my mind and my heart so that when these fires come, I know that You are with me and that You will bring me through unscathed. I love you. Amen.

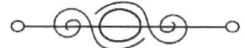

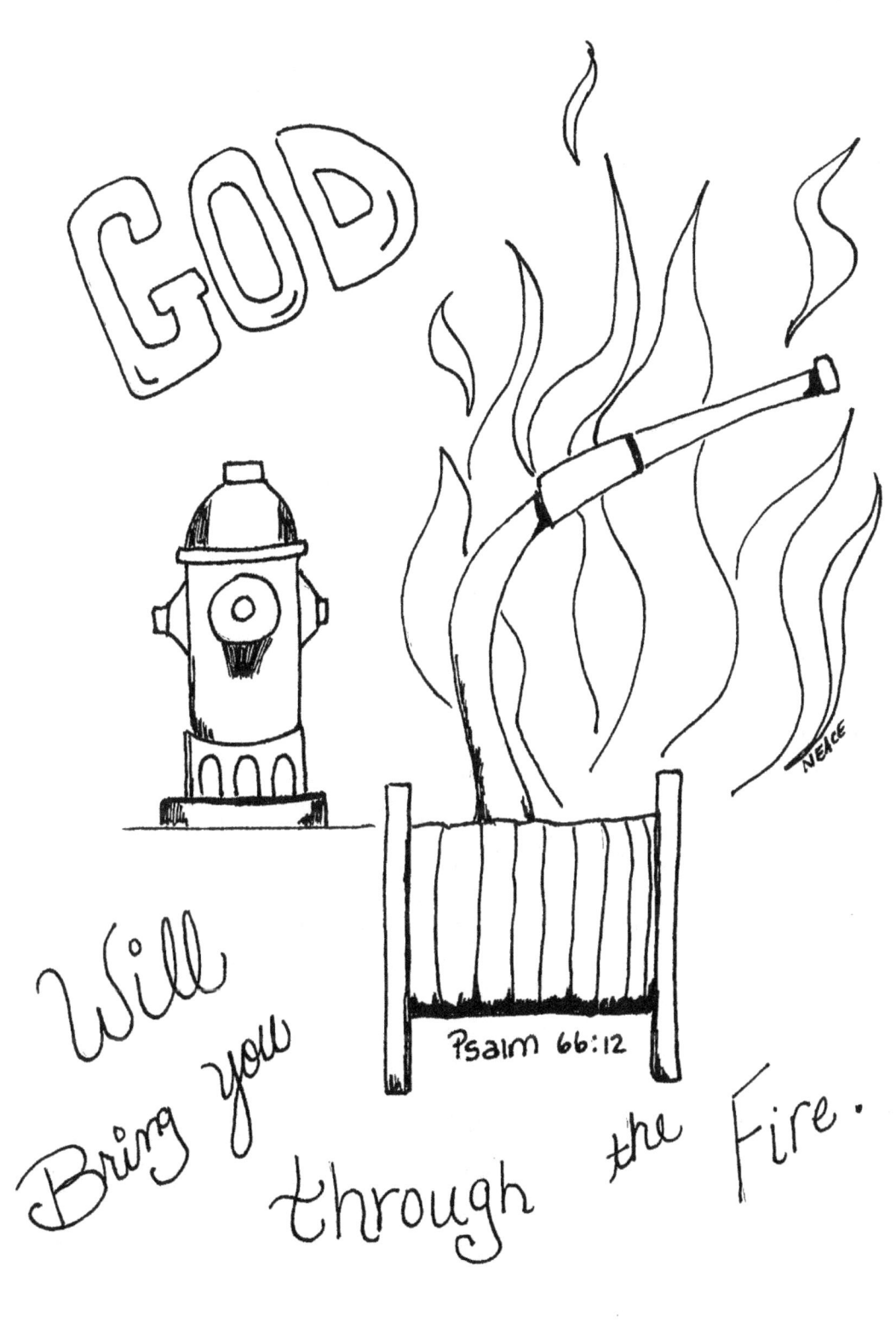

Bravery...

It takes a special person to be a first responder. Simply put, these are men and women who have feelings and emotions just like everyone else, but there is something unique that drives them to do what they do. One of the outstanding characteristics we see in these folks is bravery. When everyone else is running away, they are the ones running towards. As soon as a call goes out, they set aside their own feelings and face the darkness head long.

Not long ago, on the remembrance day of September 11th, my husband and I sat in awe as we watched video footage of the Twin Tower tragedy unfold. Countless civilians ran for their lives, coughing, choking, crying…trying to make sense of this new reality. However, time and again, firefighters, police, EMT's ran towards the towers, never giving a second thought to the destruction which awaited them.

Bravery is not something that can be taught, but rather something instilled within us deep in the recesses of our soul. And, at those special moments when all humanity is in desperate need of someone to swoop in and stop the chaos, that instinct kicks into high gear with our first responders. May God continue to wrap His ever loving arms around them as they fight the good fight.

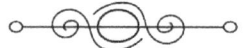

Bravery is being scared to death and gearing up anyway.

Have I not commanded you? Be strong and courageous. Do not be afraid; do not be discouraged, for the LORD your God will be with you wherever you go. –Joshua 1:9

Strong and Courageous…

Joshua in the Bible was a great leader – a man who understood his mission and saw to it that it was carried out. However, as we all do at times, he experienced a moment of weakness. What a grand opportunity for God to remind Joshua that he operated in God's strength, not his own.

Today, there will be times we become so focused on our weaknesses. We may even ask, "Who am I to do this or that?" Yet, that is exactly where God wants us. It is there He can do His best work - when we are empty of ourselves yet full of Him. Be strong and courageous, warrior. He will be with you!

Dear Heavenly Father,
Give me courage and strength today in the tasks that are at hand. Whether I am a spouse at home or a first responder helping those who are facing some of their darkest moments, give me exactly what I need today. Thank You for being with me.
Amen.

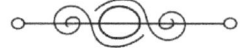

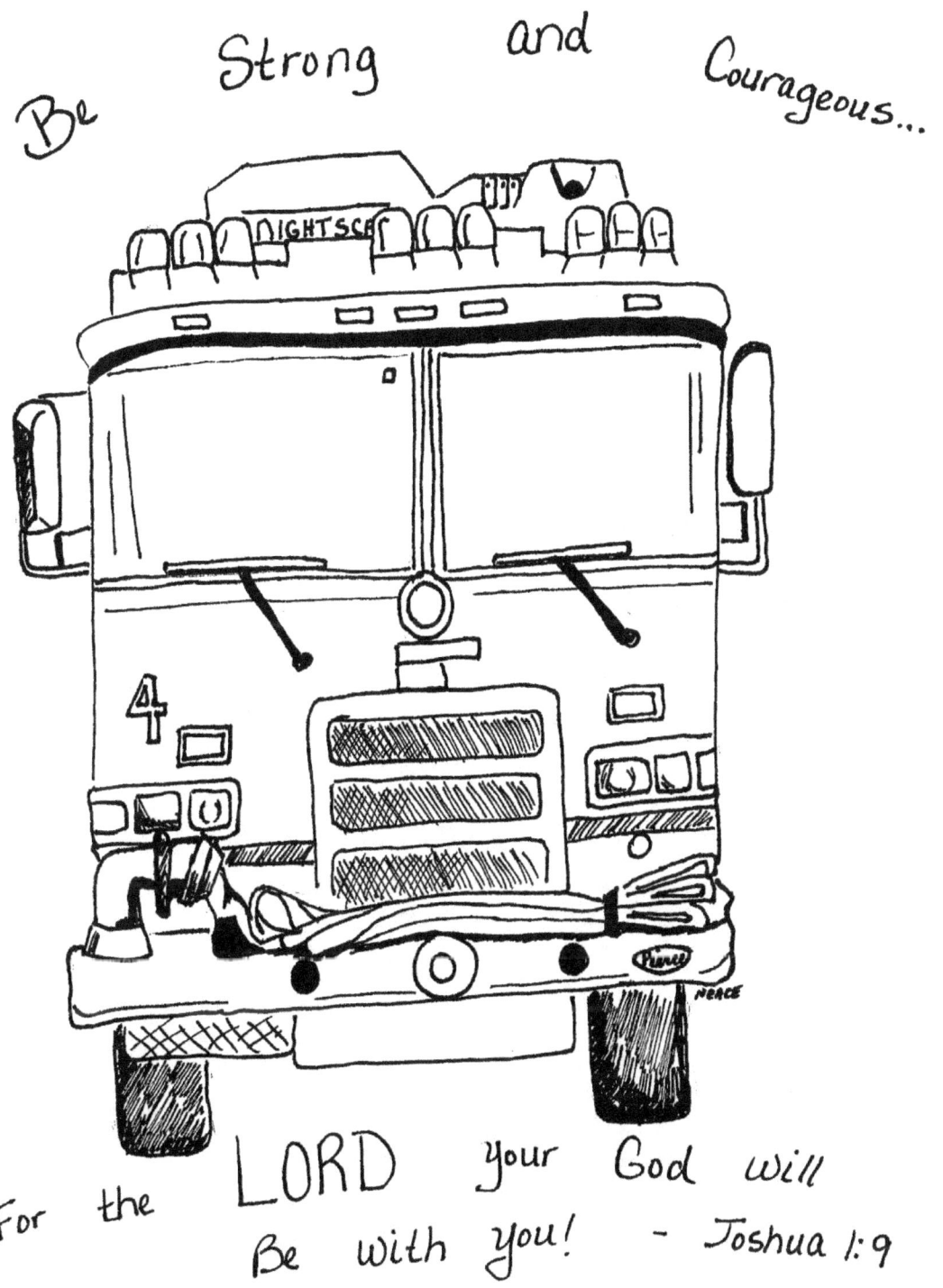

Together as One!...

There are moments when first responders – whether police, fire, or EMS, communications etc., become exclusive in their area of service. Yet, we must remind ourselves that together we serve on the same team and make up a special force of individuals who bring help to the hurting, calmness to the chaos, and a quick response to those who are facing loss. Each one has a unique role. Each one has a vital part to play. And, when we work as one well-oiled machine, countless lives are touched. Sounds like something the Lord might have His hand on, doesn't it? Thank you all for your service!

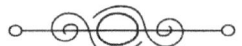

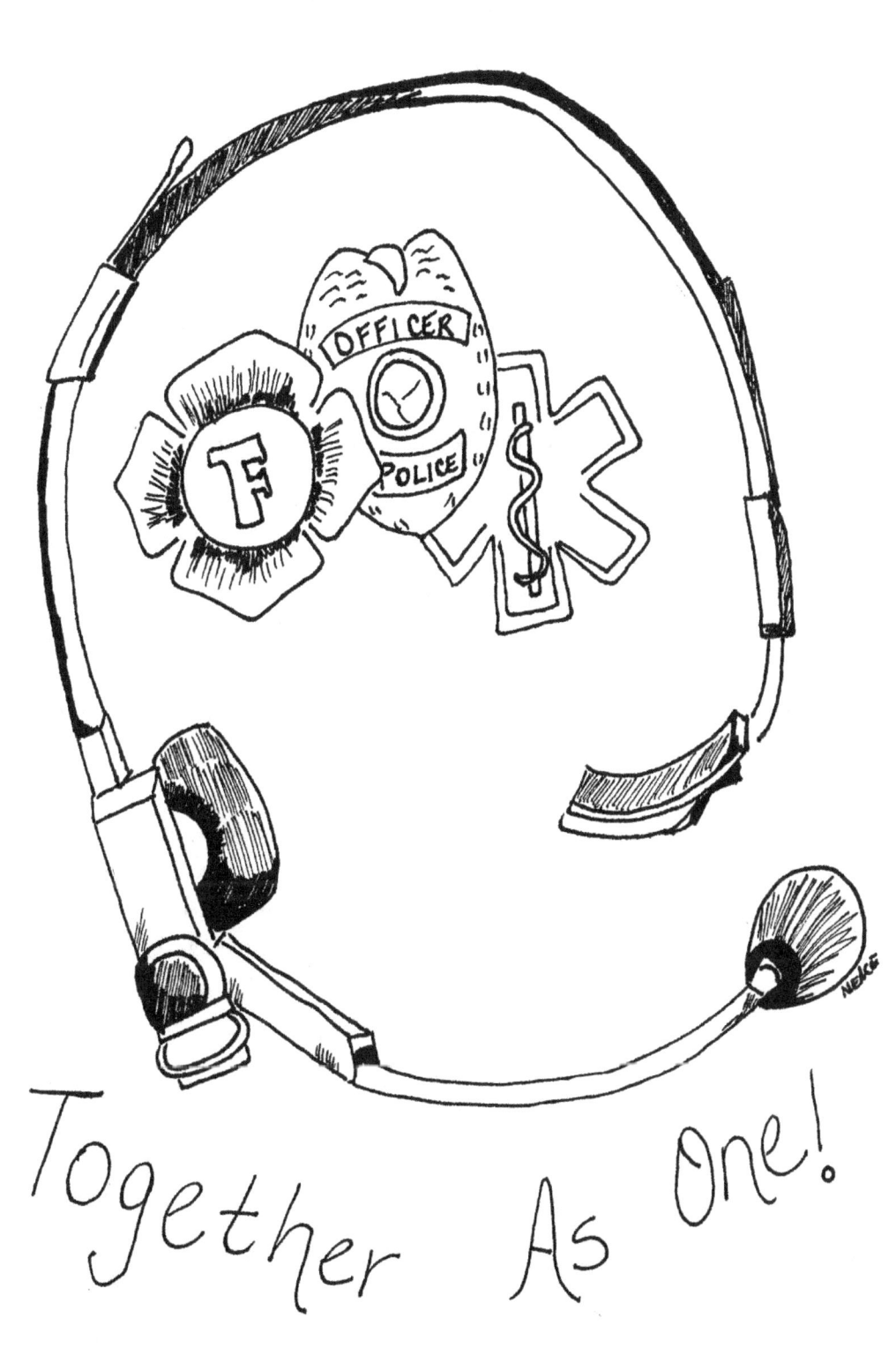

A Full Moon Can Be Terrifying!...

As I type that statement I laugh a bit to myself, thinking back to the countless conversations my husband and I have had when noting a full moon. For whatever reason and whatever the cause, it seems that those nights when the light shines brightest, all hell breaks loose. Why is that?

Of course, I see it through a spiritual lens. When God is doing the most visible work in a person's life, that is also the time the enemy fights hardest against him or her. Whether the moonlight has any pull or effect on people's human nature, I cannot say, but what I do know is that in His infinite wisdom and mercy, God provides those special servants to help combat the upswing of negativity and alarm. In our own lives, when God moves in vibrant and visible ways, and the enemy is fighting hard against, often there are people placed there to offer an encouraging word or thoughtful deed to help us through those times.

I am grateful for our first responders who battle the demons of the night, but I am equally grateful for those blessed individuals whom God sends our way to help refocus our eyes back on Him.

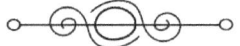

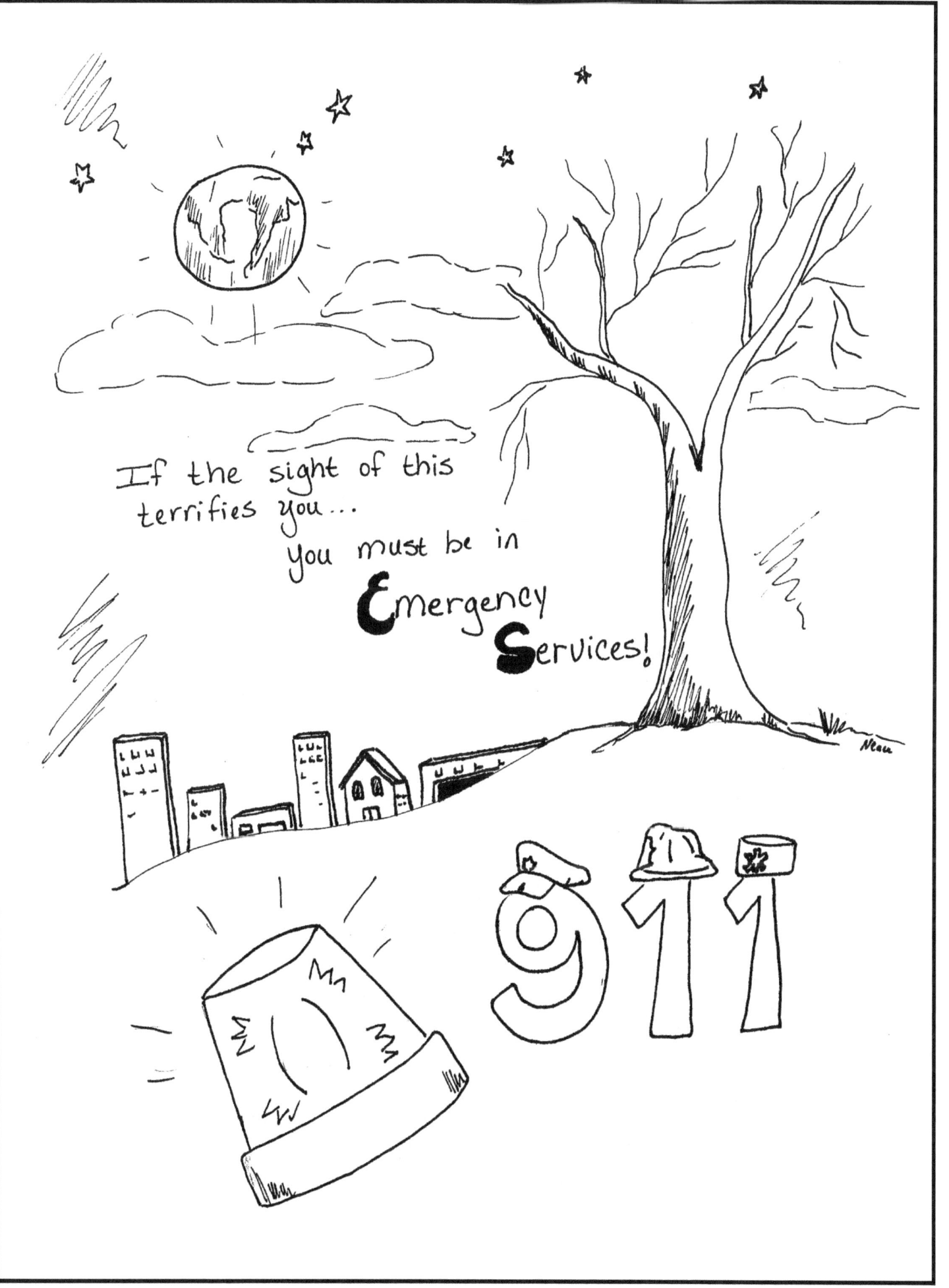

About the Author and Artist, Kristi Neace

Kristi is an author, speaker and artist. She has been married to her officer husband for almost 30 years. Together, Kristi and husband, Rick, have raised three children, one of whom is an officer, along with a son-in-law who also serves in law enforcement. Currently they reside in Missouri, but travel extensively with their non-profit, Badge of Hope Ministries.

Badge of Hope Ministries exists to come alongside those struggling with marital issues, job stress, PTSD, spiritual issues, etc. They also enjoy blessing officers/families through projects such as lunch with LEOs, Thanks-for-Giving baskets, Shop with a Cop, Officer Appreciation Events, Scholarships, meals, and so much more!

For more information, please visit: **www.badgeofhopeministries.com**
Also, be sure to check out Kristi's extensive list of books on Amazon.